text: Peter Terrell
illustrations: Elfreda Crehan

Published 2019 by Lexus Ltd
47 Broad Street, Glasgow G40 2QW

©Lexus Ltd, 2019

All rights reserved. No part of this publication may be reproduced or stored in any form without permission from Lexus Ltd, except for the use of short sections in reviews.

www.lexusforlanguages.co.uk

British Library Cataloguing in Publication Data

A catalogue record for this book is available from the British Library.

ISBN: 9781904737551

Thanks to Nathalie Chalmers for reading the French

Printed and bound in Bulgaria by PULSIO PRINT

a love-hate relationship 5

screen screen screen 24

magic app of the future 45

a love – hate relationship

je l'aime et je le déteste

my phone's my friend, but not the best

il veut toujours que je le regarde

and saying no is not that hard

le respect de votre vie privée est notre priorité

désolé, je suis occupé

and a hundred selfies every day

parfois je pense, assez, assez

à vrai dire, tu sais, ça m'emmerde

all these photos that must get shared

but still there's sometimes inner peace
musique, jeux et calculatrice

et c'est toi, mon ami, qui m'as sauvé la vie

when once a loo door slammed shut on me

quand la belle plage s'est transformée en île

you've called a thousand times before

laissez-moi un message après le bip sonore

mobile phone, you're the best

oui, je t'aime... et oui je te déteste

screen screen screen

screen screen screen

tu sais que tu domines

plus personne n'est vraiment là

it's just their bodies where they are

are the others really there?

les amoureux ne se regardent guère

les couples mariés pas du tout

they've much more tempting things to do

kids go out with mum and dad

vite, donne-lui donc son petit iPad

driving home after the meal

SMS au volant ? c'est pas difficile

tu veux te faire tuer, espèce d'idiot !!!

who's that dozy so and so!

oui oui chéri, je suis en route

why can't these tourists hear me hoot?

it's just their bodies where they are

plus personne n'est vraiment là

tu sais que tu domines
screen screen screen

magic app of the future

il s'est passé quelque chose

where it came from no-one knows

this totally amazing app, ok
sans le savoir, je l'ai téléchargée.

cette appli d'une puissance si forte
that taught my phone to teleport

now I just zip across the sky

partout où je veux que mes particules s'en aillent

je n'ai qu'à déclencher cette appli

and there's nowhere I can't quickly be

other people stand and stare

tiens, un remontage moléculaire !

le métro plein ? les routes bloquées ?

zap zap, my lovely little app
emmène-moi, il faut qu'on s'échappe

en un rien de temps, ah oui, c'est bizarre !
I'm re-assembled in the bar

enfin, c'était trop beau pour être vrai

flat battery had the final say

once when I was just halfway there

j'ai eu une panne ... moléculaire